Pebble® Plus

GW01395783

Science Tools

Microscopes AND Magnifying Glasses

Lisa J. Amstutz

raintree

a Capstone company — publishers for children

Raintree is an imprint of Capstone Global Library Limited, a company incorporated in England and Wales having its registered office at 264 Banbury Road, Oxford, OX2 7DY – Registered company number: 6695582

www.raintree.co.uk
myorders@raintree.co.uk

Edited by Anna Butzer
Designed by Cynthia Della-Rovere
Picture research by Kelly Garvin
Production by Tori Abraham
Originated by Capstone Global Library Limited

ISBN 978 1 4747 6932 7 (hardback)
ISBN 978 1 4747 6950 1 (paperback)

British Library Cataloguing in Publication Data
A full catalogue record for this book is available from the British Library

Acknowledgements
We would like to thank the following for permission to reproduce photographs: Capstone Press/Karon Dubke, cover, 1 (top left), 15, 19, 21; iStockphoto: FatCamera, 5,17, JLBarranco, 9; Shutterstock: Dargon Images, 11, Galileo30, 1 (bottom right), Nenad Zivkovic, 3, Purino, 7, Triff, 13. Design elements: Shutterstock: Alina G, Astarina, Fafarumba, happy_fox_art, Lorelyn Medina, mhatzapa, Netkoff, Nikitina Karina, olllikeballoon, PedroNevesDesign, Visual Generation.

Every effort has been made to contact copyright holders of material reproduced in this book. Any omissions will be rectified in subsequent printings if notice is given to the publisher.

All the internet addresses (URLs) given in this book were valid at the time of going to press. However, due to the dynamic nature of the internet, some addresses may have changed, or sites may have changed or ceased to exist since publication. While the author and publisher regret any inconvenience this may cause readers, no responsibility for any such changes can be accepted by either the author or the publisher.

Printed and bound in India

Contents

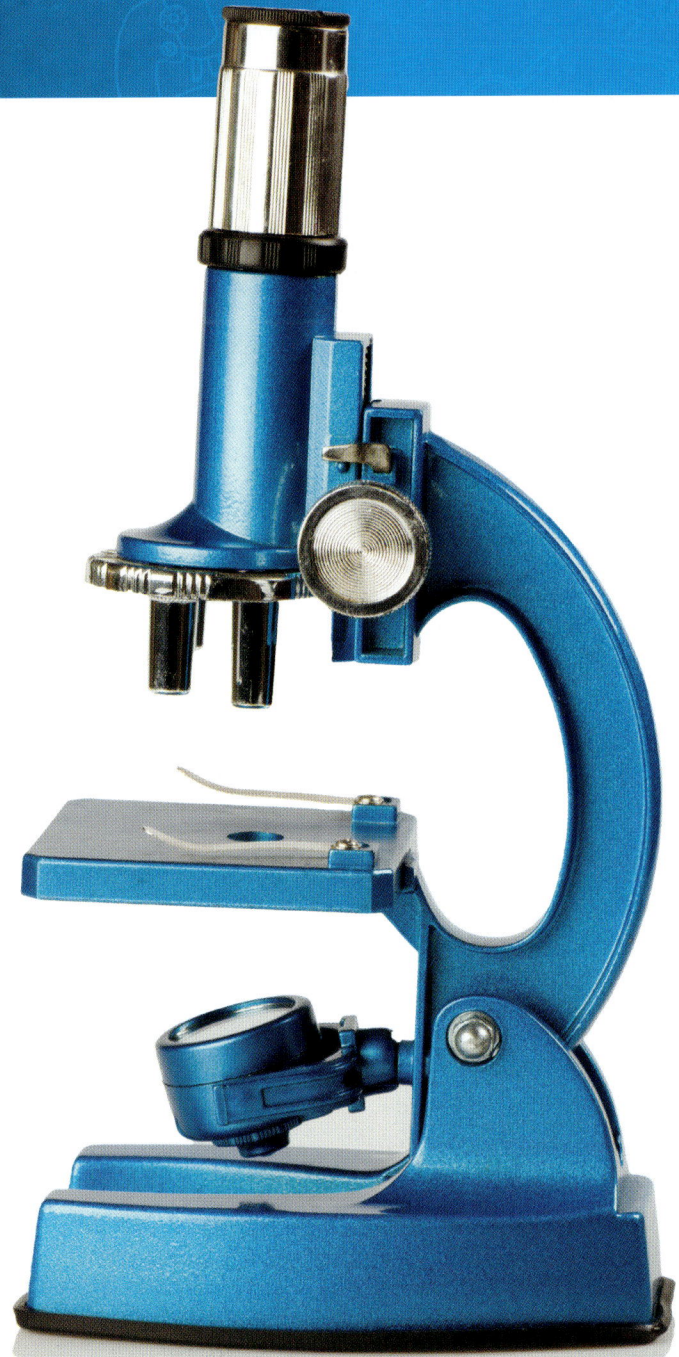

What is a Magnifying Glass?

The world is full of tiny things. Some things are too small for our eyes to see. A microscope or magnifying glass can help!

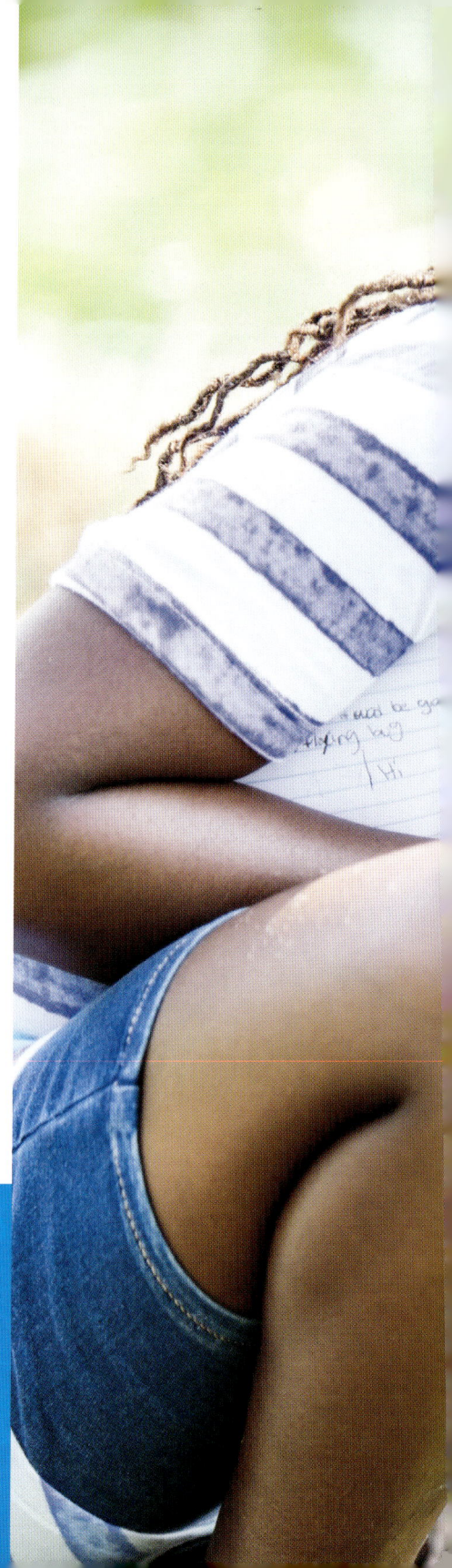

A magnifying glass has a curved piece of glass in it. It bends light. When you look through it, objects look bigger than they are.

LOOK CLOSER

A magnifying glass is small and easy to carry. You can put it in a backpack and carry it around.

Find a leaf or a flower. Hold the magnifying glass close to your eye. Bring the leaf towards the glass. It should look bigger. A magnifying glass can make things look up to 20 times bigger.

What is a Microscope?

A microscope has a
lens tube with two lenses.
The lens you look through
is called the eyepiece. The other
lens is called the objective.

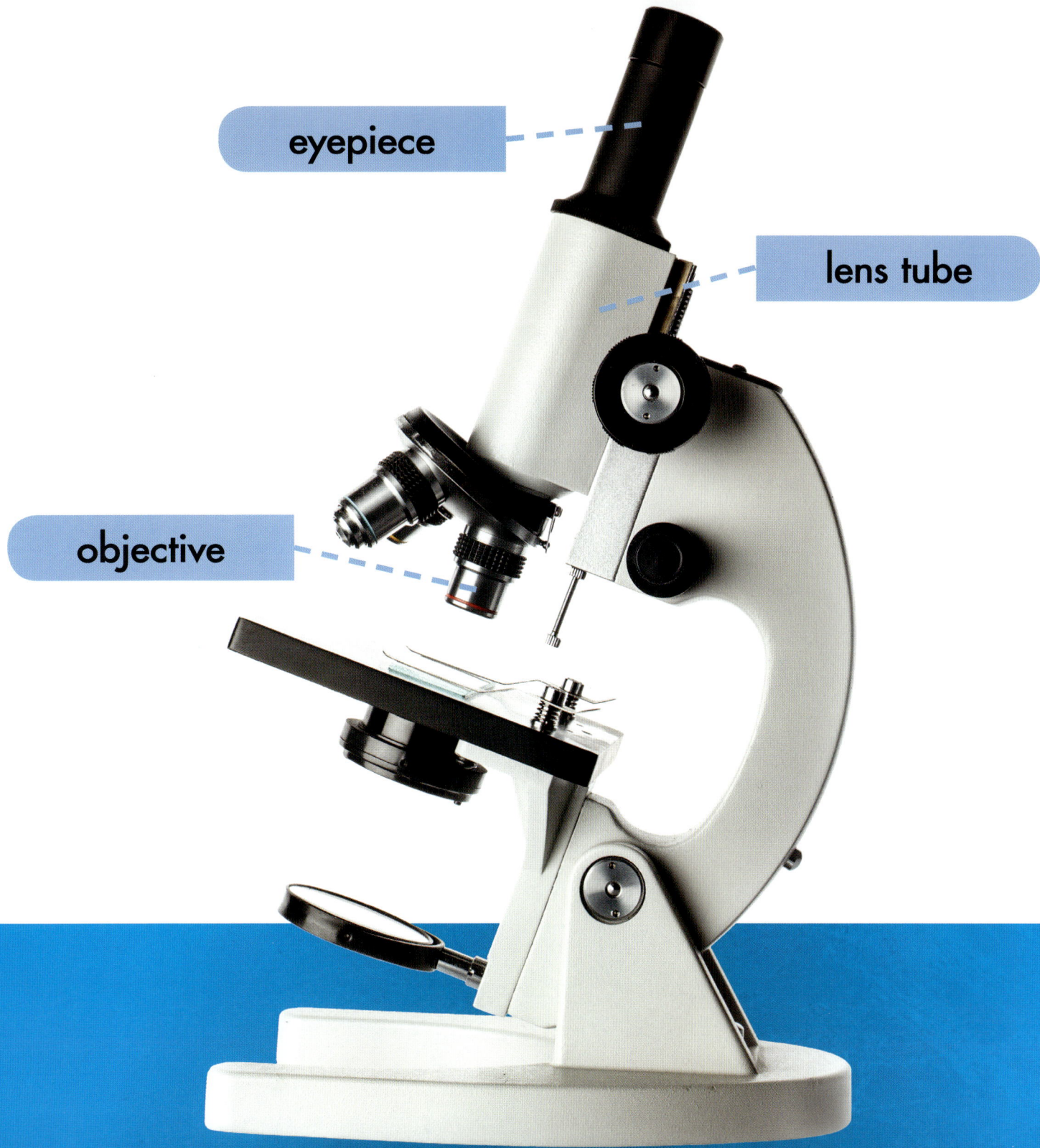

eyepiece

lens tube

objective

A microscope can magnify up to 1,500 times. Place a piece of hair on a slide. Put a slide cover on top. Then clip the slide onto the stage.

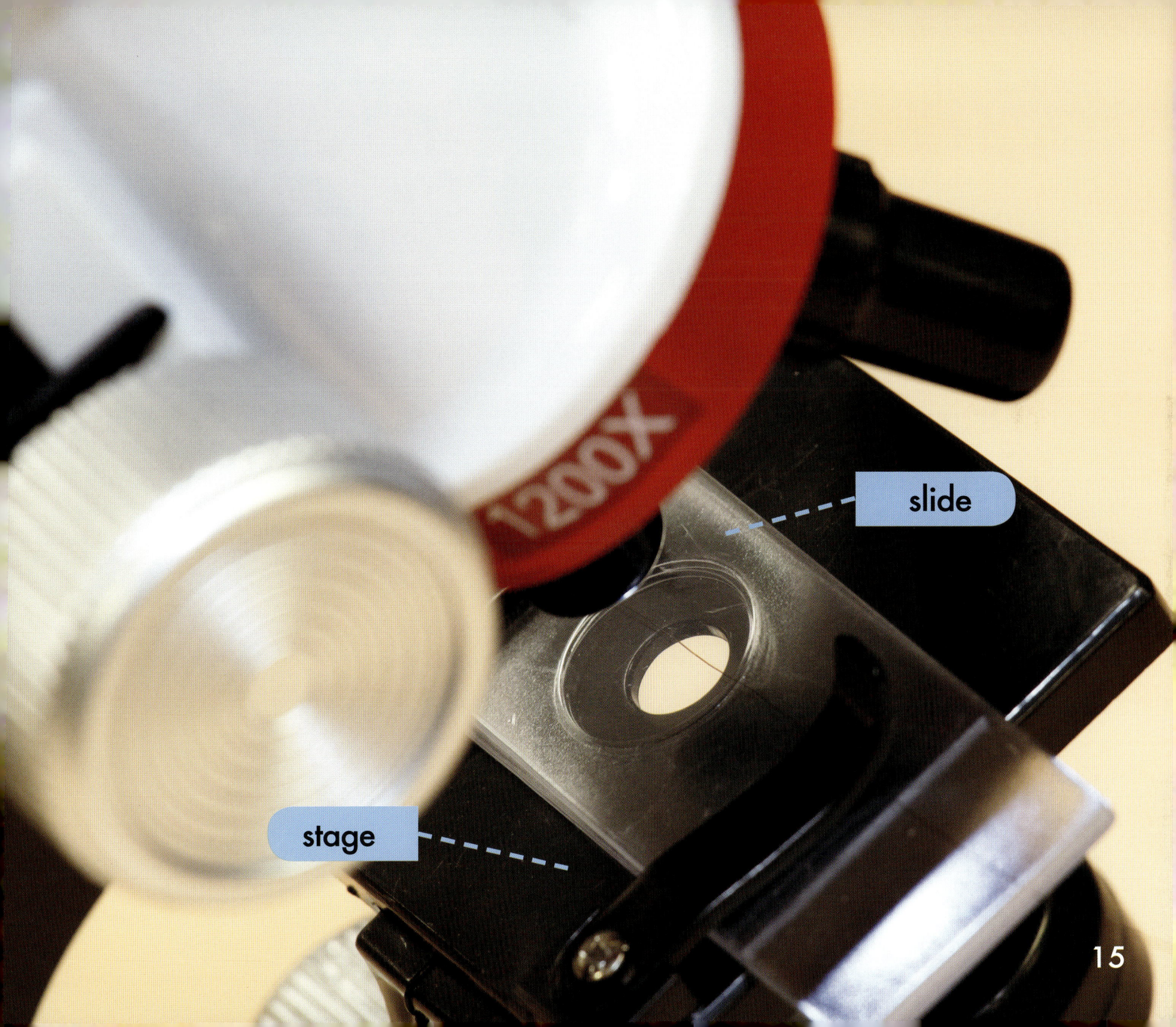

slide

stage

15

Look into the tube to see the hair. Two knobs focus the microscope. They move the lens tube up and down. Another knob moves the stage.

knob

Safety first!

Many lenses are made of glass. They can break easily. Use both hands to pick up a microscope. Put one hand under the base. That way you will not drop it.

Microscopes and magnifying glasses help scientists to study things closely. What new things can you discover with a lens?

Glossary

base the lowest part of something, or the part that it stands on

eyepiece a curved piece of glass in a microscope that you look through

focus to make a clear image

magnify to make something look larger than it really is

objective lens in a microscope made of a curved piece of glass; it collects light and magnifies an image

slide a small piece of glass that holds an object so it can be seen under a microscope

stage a platform on a microscope that holds a slide

Find out more

Complete Book of the Microscope, Kirsteen Rogers (Usborne Publishing Ltd, 2012)

How to Measure Everything: A Fun First Guide to the Maths of Measuring, DK (DK Children, 2018)

Websites

DK Findout! Facts on miscroscopes
www.dkfindout.com/uk/science/microscopes/

Easy Science for Kids: All about microscopes
easyscienceforkids.com/all-about-microscopes/

INDEX